What Is God's Mission in the World

and How Do We Join It?

"I don't how they've done it, but Juan Martínez and Jamie Pitts have condensed what previous missiologists have taken hundreds of pages to do—namely, explain the whole of the Christian mission. This little book contains all you need to know about God's mission and how to join it. It should be distributed like tracts at every church and seminary!"

—**AL TIZON**, affiliate associate professor of missional and global leadership at North Park University

"Grounded in a confident humility rooted in God's purposes for humanity and for the whole of creation, Martínez and Pitts present a compelling articulation of the role of the church in God's mission in the way of Jesus. This brief, yet comprehensive, book should be read by everyone interested in mission."

—**STANLEY W. GREEN**, former president and executive director for Mennonite Mission Network

"Concise, contemporary, and written from a multi-cultural perspective, Martínez and Pitts walk us through Jesus-centric mission, the pros and cons of our mission history, the God-ordained purpose of the church, and the challenge of incarnational living. A must-read for pastors or leaders working to heal our cultural divides."

—**PAUL BORTHWICK**, author of *Western Christians in Global Mission: What's the Role of the North American Church?*

"Martínez and Pitts invite us to reexamine the essence of God's mission for this moment in history through the incarnational model of Jesus. They substantially cover the theological, historical, ecclesial, and social dimensions of Christ-centered mission and remind us that the invitation to join the Jesus way continues to be the same. A valuable book."

—**SUE PARK-HUR**, Mennonite Church USA

THE JESUS WAY
—SMALL BOOKS *of* RADICAL FAITH—

What Is God's Mission in the World

and How Do We Join It?

JUAN FRANCISCO MARTÍNEZ & JAMIE PITTS

Herald
PRESS

Harrisonburg, Virginia

Herald Press
PO Box 866, Harrisonburg, Virginia 22803
www.HeraldPress.com

Study guides are available for many Herald Press titles at www.HeraldPress.com.

WHAT IS GOD'S MISSION IN THE WORLD AND HOW DO WE JOIN IT?
© 2021 by Herald Press, Harrisonburg, Virginia 22803. 800-245-7894.
    All rights reserved.
Library of Congress Control Number: 2020052708
International Standard Book Number: 978-1-5138-0566-5 (paperback);
    978-1-5138-0615-0 (ebook)
Printed in United States of America
Cover and interior design by Reuben Graham

25 24 23 22 21   10 9 8 7 6 5 4 3 2 1

Contents

Introduction to The Jesus Way Series from Herald Press

The Jesus Way is good news for all people, of all times, in all places. Jesus Christ "is before all things, and in him all things hold together"; "in him all the fullness of God was pleased to dwell" (Colossians 1:17, 19). The Jesus Way happens when God's will is done on earth as it is in heaven.

But what does it mean to walk the Jesus Way? How can we who claim the name of Christ reflect the image of God in the twenty-first century? What does it mean to live out and proclaim the good news of reconciliation in Christ?

The Jesus Way: Small Books of Radical Faith offers concise, practical theology that helps readers encounter big questions about God's work in the world. Grounded in a Christ-centered reading of Scripture and a commitment to reconciliation, the series aims to enliven the service and embolden the witness of people who follow Jesus. The volumes in the series are written by a diverse community of internationally renowned pastors, scholars, and practitioners committed to the way of Jesus.

The Jesus Way series is rooted in Anabaptism, a Christian tradition that prioritizes following Jesus, loving enemies, and creating faithful communities. During the Protestant Reformation of the 1500s, early Anabaptists who began meeting for worship emphasized discipleship in addition to belief, baptized adults instead of infants, and pledged their allegiance to God over loyalty to the state. Early Anabaptists were martyred for their radical faith, and they went to their deaths without violently resisting their accusers.

Today more than two million Anabaptist Christians worship in more than one hundred countries around the globe. They include Mennonites, Amish, Brethren in Christ, and Hutterites. Many other Christians committed to Anabaptist beliefs and practices remain in church communities in other traditions.

Following Jesus means turning from sin, renouncing violence, seeking justice, believing in the reconciling power of God, and living in the power of the Holy Spirit. The Jesus Way liberates us from conformity to the world and heals broken places. It shines light on evil and restores all things.

Join Christ-followers around the world as we seek the Jesus Way.

Introduction

What is the point of Christian faith? What is the point of the church? One of the ways to answer these questions has been to use the language of **mission**.[1] But for many that word has come to be associated with the worst parts of Christianity. It brings up a legacy of ignorance, manipulation, and violence. It brings up a legacy of colonialism and white supremacy. Since those legacies are alive and well today—as seen in the sickening convergence of white nationalism and science denialism in many churches—it may seem better to leave behind "mission" and everything it represents.

We are sympathetic to these concerns about the language of Christian mission, and spend part of this book reckoning with the atrocities committed in the name of mission. At the same time, we find the language of mission unavoidable. God is at work in the world and calls us to join that work. Responding to God's call, through the power of the Holy Spirit, is the point of Christian faith. It is the point of the church. "Mission," at its best, names our fallible, developing understanding of our purpose and task as Christians. "Mission" names our often misguided attempts to participate in God's loving care of the world.

Christians have been involved in mission since the time of the New Testament. Though they have used many different methods, some deserving to be lauded and others condemned, most churches agree that their reason to exist is God's mission, to join in God's action and purposes in the world. Because of Christian mission throughout the centuries there are now churches in most cultures, ethnicities, and language groups around the world. But Christian churches have not always had a similar understanding of the task at hand. Different Christian traditions focus on different biblical texts and theological framings to define what mission means to them. Sometimes the differences seem somewhat minor and sometimes they are clearly profound.

In this book, we want to start with Jesus, and not merely with his final commands to his disciples before leaving them and returning to his Father's presence (the great commission of Matthew 28:18-20). By looking at the whole of the person, work, teachings, and spirit of Jesus, our understanding of what God is doing in the world expands. This book will constantly invite the reader to a broader vision of what God is doing and what the church needs to be doing as it practices mission in the way of Jesus. We believe that this broader vision directly challenges the racist, imperialistic Christianity that is wreaking havoc on our world.

We will begin by focusing on the incarnation as a key factor in understanding the mission of Jesus (chapter 1). The Jesus Way, we suggest in this series, means understanding all aspects of our lives—in this case, mission—by looking at Jesus as the clearest example of what God is doing in the world. The second chapter will provide a short introduction to the history of Christian mission, to how Christians have understood and attempted mission, and to some of the questions about mission that have arisen over time. The third chapter focuses on the church as the missional community. Mission is lived out by Christians who are part of concrete communities of faith, enacting their commitment to Jesus Christ together. Chapter 4 focuses on what incarnational mission looks like in the world today. What does it look like to be involved in a Jesus Way mission? The final chapter addresses some of the important questions that Christians need to address as they seek to be faithful to the task. For example, how do we talk about the uniqueness of Jesus in interreligious or post-Christian environments? Or, what does Christian witness look like in a time of racist violence, ecological crisis, and global pandemic?

An understanding of mission in the Jesus Way gives the task a specific orientation and direction. Other Christians will start from other perspectives and give the concept of mission a slightly, or profoundly, different focus. Focusing on Jesus does not mean that this is a perfect way or the only significant way to understand mission. But this perspective can provide an important contribution to the church at large as it seeks to be faithful to God's call. So you are invited to this way of understanding God's mission—but most importantly you are invited to join what God is doing in the world by following the Jesus Way.

1

God's Mission Looks like Jesus

And the Word became flesh and lived among us, and we have seen his glory, the glory as of a father's only son, full of grace and truth.
—John 1:14

John Perkins grew up in an African American sharecropper family in rural Mississippi. After the racially motivated murder of his older brother, Perkins relocated to California for his own safety, married Vera Mae Buckley, and began a ministry. When he returned to Mississippi, he came to see that preaching the **gospel** required economic and political solidarity with the poor. Perkins was arrested and tortured for his civil rights activism in the 1960s, but remained steadfast in his vision, calling affluent Christians to move into impoverished

urban neighborhoods and work alongside the poor for economic justice and spiritual and social reconciliation.

One fruit of Perkins's teaching is Servant Partners, a ministry based in Southern California and active in over twenty
cities worldwide. Servant Partners workers carry on Perkins's
vision of ministry with (not *to* or *for*) the poor by relocating to
their neighborhoods and empowering them for leadership in
their communities. Like Perkins, Servant Partners takes Jesus'
incarnate solidarity with the poor as its primary model.

One of the key doctrines of Christian faith is the **incarnation**.
In this confession, believers state that God became a human to
be able to address the human condition. It is not only that God
was concerned about humans and sent Jesus. The confession is
much more radical. God became a part of humanity, and fully
entered the human condition, in the person of Jesus. Jesus is
God's way of being human.

This confession has powerful implications for the Jesus
Way understanding of mission. Jesus is God incarnate. But he
is also God's mission incarnate. If we want to understand what
God is about in the world, Jesus provides us with the clearest
indication. Incarnation is a fundamental part of what God is
doing and how God is working.

That is why Jesus Way mission begins with the incarnation. Any attempt to share Jesus' message as good news has to
follow the path of the incarnation. That means, on individual
and communal levels, striving to imitate Jesus' solidarity with
the poor, the imprisoned, and others marginalized by society.
Incarnational solidarity in the Jesus Way means taking up
Jesus' mission of healing and liberation as central to our own
lives. We can only take up that mission alongside—not above
or outside of—the communities Jesus seeks to heal and liberate.

To come alongside a group of people requires deep respect for their language, culture, and society, and for their own analysis of their situation. It requires a willingness to share their ways of life, including their celebrations and hardships, as they invite us to do so. And it requires great sensitivity to how our well-intentioned presence may actually make things worse for them. Aligning our mission with Jesus gives us a positive task, as well as an awareness of how our efforts can go wrong.

Since Jesus is God's mission incarnate, then understanding the person, teachings, and work of Jesus frames the Jesus Way view of mission. In some popular evangelistic perspectives, the focus is on the work of Christ on the cross. A review of the whole of Jesus' life broadens that perspective and provides a crucial way to understand God's mission and the church's task in the world.

The gospel writers' first descriptions of Jesus' life have to do with an incarnation in the broadest sense of the word. God becomes flesh. But Jesus incarnates into a continuing saga. He is a part of a people who have been invited to be a source of God's blessing for all humanity (Genesis 12). He is a part of a specific family of people, first called Israelites and later Jews, who are open to what God is doing.

The birth narratives also connect Jesus with many people (like Simeon and Anna) who are expecting the coming of God's sent one. The Gospels present us committed women (Mary and Elizabeth) willing to literally be the means of incarnation and of bringing the Messiah and his herald into the world. The story includes faithful outsiders (the magi, or astrologers) who travel from afar to worship the newborn child. Angels share the wonderful news with marginalized people (shepherds) able and willing to accept the message. But the message also points to opposition and indifference to the Jesus mission. The

Messiah is the sent one. But he is also the persecuted one from the beginning of his earthly life.

Each of the gospel writers points to a different specific moment in describing Jesus' first steps into public ministry. The one that contains the most elaborate declaration of purpose and mission is the scene in Luke 4, when Jesus quotes Isaiah 61 to describe his mission.

> He unrolled the scroll and found the place where it was written:
>
>> "The Spirit of the Lord is upon me,
>>   because he has anointed me
>>   to bring good news to the poor.
>> He has sent me to proclaim release to the captives
>>   and recovery of sight to the blind,
>>   to let the oppressed go free,
>> to proclaim the year of the Lord's favor."
>
> And he rolled up the scroll, gave it back to the attendant, and sat down. The eyes of all in the synagogue were fixed on him. Then he began to say to them, "Today this scripture has been fulfilled in your hearing." (Luke 4:17-21)

By using this portion of Isaiah as his declaration, Jesus is doing several things. He is placing himself in the ongoing narrative of God's work in the world. Jesus is declaring that he is the anointed one, the Messiah who has been foretold in the Hebrew Scriptures. He is also stating that his mission has broad implications for humans and that he is proclaiming God's **shalom** and jubilee, God's reign of peace and freedom for all. Jesus' message, in other words, is for all peoples, for "all the families of the earth" (Genesis 12:3), including those who have historically been the enemies of the Jews. And that is something that some of those present are not ready to accept.

So Luke lets us know that even as Jesus proclaims his earthly task, the crowd rejects the implications and tries to kill him.

Jesus' ministry and teachings are a living-out of the proclamation he made in Luke 4. He addresses the needs of the poor, the captives, the blind, and the oppressed. His miracles are truly good news to the poor, to the marginalized, to the needy of society. The healings provide hope and a future for those who have no access to the medical care available at the time. The miraculous feedings address the hunger that many of the poor constantly face. During his earthly ministry, Jesus often confronts those with power who are using it to keep people captive. Jesus also offers grace to those whose **sin** has separated them from society and confronts those who consider themselves too good to need God's grace.

The teachings of Jesus focus on the alternative reality that God wants to develop through Jesus. One author has called it "the upside-down kingdom."[1] Jesus turns the values of his society, and of others, on their head. The poor are blessed, and the rich are turned away. The Sermon on the Mount (Matthew 5–7) is a declaration of the radical values of the gospel and an invitation to "seek first the kingdom of God and his righteousness" (Matthew 6:33 ESV). Jesus invites his followers to be peacemakers, to be willing to suffer for his cause when necessary, to love their enemies, to bless those that curse them, and to find creative, nonviolent ways to subvert and resist oppressive powers rather than imitating their quest for violent domination. Jesus constantly upends the values of his society, and ours. Jesus invites his hearers to reject the "blessings" of the empire and to seek the blessing of God by living the values of God's upside-down kingdom.

Jesus also confronts the religious legalism that had developed in his day. Because the good news of God's reign is for those who recognize that they need a doctor (Luke 5:31), Jesus often finds himself at odds with those most dedicated to being faithful to God's law. Jesus presents his listeners with two radical notions that many people see as being in conflict.

Jesus claims that the radical grace of God is for all, including those who have wandered farthest from the way of righteousness, like the prodigal son (Luke 15:11-32). This is why Jesus hangs out with the sinners and marginalized of his time—to help them see that they can enjoy restored relations with God and their communities. But Jesus does not offer cheap grace; he does not downplay the seriousness of sin or deny moral responsibility. That is why Jesus forgives peoples' sin and invites them to "go your way, and from now on do not sin again" (John 8:11). The legalists want their faithfulness to be the basis for their acceptance before God, but Jesus constantly reminds them that God's grace is the same for all. God's healing, restorative, and empowering embrace is offered to all, regardless of individual merit.

Jesus' teachings also focus on the kingdom, the reign of God. This is an invitation into a new order, one that looks radically different from human political and social structures. The gospel is about the forgiveness of personal sins; it is about how God is present to enable each of us to live more like Jesus. But it is about much more than personal transformation.

God is bringing the future into the present. God is inviting people to live into the future reign of God today. Jesus' miracles are a foretaste of that future, a future of healing and abundance for all of God's creation. His teachings point his followers toward how to live into that future today. The parables in particular become teaching tools that invite people to understand the beauty and the complexity of living into God's future today. Amid our struggles to live into God's future,

Jesus' teachings constantly press on us the question, Whose blessing do you want—God's or empire's?

In the gospel of John, Jesus refers to himself as "I am" to point to what God is doing through him. Jesus is "the bread of life," "the light of the world," "the door," "the good shepherd," "the resurrection and the life," "the way, the truth and the life," and "the true vine." These analogies and references point both to who Jesus is, the "I Am" of the Hebrew Scriptures (Exodus 3:14)—the mysterious source of all things who comes to be known through concrete acts of social and political liberation, and also to the provision with which God nurtures humanity. Jesus' mission is to provide humanity with its profoundly basic needs of sustenance, freedom, community, direction, and life abundant and eternal.

A Jesus Way understanding of mission looks at the whole of Jesus' life and teachings. But a key part of his work is his death and resurrection. How are we to understand the connection between his suffering and what God is doing in the world? How does it fit into our understanding of mission? The New Testament addresses this issue at many levels, particularly in describing the work of Jesus in light of the **atonement** of sin from the legal code of the Old Testament. Jesus is the Lamb of God who takes away the sin of the world (John 1:29). But what is the connection between Jesus' death on the cross and God's work in the world?

Christians have attempted to interpret the significance of Jesus' death and resurrection using what are often called theories of the atonement. The three most prominent theories in Western Christianity are *Christus Victor*, substitutionary atonement, and moral influence. Each of these have been taught by different Christian theologians for centuries. These theories each point toward one aspect of what Jesus did, and—as theories or general, self-sufficient accounts of the work of Christ—they often make that particular aspect normative in how they understand the work of Christ. Each looks at the death and resurrection of Jesus and understands their significance differently.

The first, *Christus Victor*, or Christ the Victor, sees the death of Jesus in terms of a battle with evil. What Jesus did on the cross was win victory over Satan, not by military or spiritual might, but through suffering and death. Satan was unable to keep Jesus from resurrecting. Christ is victorious so that we can be free from the power of sin and evil.

The second theory, substitutionary atonement, focuses on Jesus as our substitute. Like the sacrifices of the Old Testament, the Lamb of God became our substitute, taking our sin upon himself so that we can be free of the punishment for our sin.

The third, moral influence theory, places the focus on the impact of Jesus' life and death on us. His teachings and his work call us to change, his death invites us to be willing to die, and his resurrection inspires us to newness of life.

In his book *Understanding the Atonement for the Mission of the Church*, author John Driver challenges us to look at the many ways the New Testament speaks about the work of Jesus Christ.[2] He argues that the atonement is so powerful and significant that it cannot be reduced to one, two, or three aspects. The New Testament uses many terms to describe the work of Jesus Christ on behalf of humans. Concepts like adoption, reconciliation, redemption, justification, sacrifice, liberation, martyrdom, and others all point to the fact that the work of Jesus is multifaceted. We confess that Christ died for us. But the significance of what he did is broad and reaches into every aspect of human existence—and indeed, into every part of creation. That is why the New Testament uses so many different concepts and analogies to describe it. If one attempts to reduce our understanding to one analogy, one can easily end up with a limited view of what God is doing and its importance for humanity.

One of the threads that runs through all the Gospels has to do with the Holy Spirit and Jesus' mission. John the Baptizer states that the one who is coming after him will baptize with Spirit and fire. When John baptizes Jesus, the Spirit descends upon Jesus and gives testimony that he is God's chosen. Once Jesus is filled with the Spirit, he is ready to go into the desert like many prophets of old and face the temptations that will test him as he prepares for his public ministry. Jesus names that anointing as he begins his public ministry (Luke 4:18). The presence of the Spirit empowers Jesus' ministry.

When Jesus gives his final instructions to his followers, he explains that the Holy Spirit is crucial for their future. "As the Father has sent me" are his words to them (John 20:21). But he makes it clear that they need to go out in the same way he did, in the power of the Holy Spirit. All of the gospel writers make it clear that Jesus promised the power of the Spirit, a power that would produce signs and wonders like those he had done. The Spirit would empower them to be witnesses and to go out to all the world with his message, continuing his mission. They were to go out and make disciples, baptizing them and teaching them to be a part of the new community. In that power his followers would see people saved—healed and restored to relationship with God and their communities—but they would also be rejected and condemned.

Related to the issue of power is that of authority. Jesus' detractors often ask the question: "On whose authority are you doing this?" Behind the scenes, one clearly sees a conflict between the power of evil and God's power to overcome evil and its damage to humanity. Jesus claims the authority and power of his Father and sends out his followers with the same authority and power. During his earthly ministry, Jesus sends out his disciples by twos, and they see how God works through them (Luke 10). God continues the mission through the community of believers formed around Jesus.

When one looks at the life and work of Jesus, one begins to comprehend the vastness of what God is doing for humanity, of God's mission in the world. Jesus is a continuation, though also the epitome, of what God is doing. He is the embodiment of God's mission and the model for the continuation of that mission. He represents the radical grace of God that invites all humans into a new social order, God's kingdom, whose values and blessings are in clear contrast to the "blessed life" offered by imperialistic human social orders.

Jesus invites those who want to follow him to receive God's grace and share it with others. He invites them to continue the project in his name, with his authority, in the power of the Holy Spirit. He sends them out to live in light of God's future reign and to invite others to also become his disciples. These new disciples will also receive power to heal, to forgive, to deal with sin, to offer transformative change to others, because God will continue the mission through them. They are to continue Jesus' mission unto the ends of the earth and until the end of time.

The book of the Acts of the Apostles and the rest of the New Testament show how the followers of Jesus sought to live out his teachings and mission, how through the Holy Spirit they sought to embrace and imitate his incarnational solidarity. Throughout the rest of this book we will focus on the implications of this incarnational mission in the Jesus Way.

2

How Christians Have Done Mission over the Centuries

But you will receive power when the Holy Spirit has come upon you; and you will be my witnesses in Jerusalem, in all Judea and Samaria, and to the ends of the earth.
  —Acts 1:8

I (Juan) grew up in a church where Acts 1:8 was considered crucial to our task as Christians. I memorized it (in Spanish) at an early age and often heard sermons based on this passage. The challenge of these sermons was for us, personally and as a congregation, to live out this call today. As I grew older I heard others call us to continue the mission of Jesus with the motto "Acts 29."[1] What I learned later as a missiologist was that the mandate given by Jesus has guided Christians to be witnesses, using many methods, some very good and some extremely problematic, at best. But Christians have gone "to the ends of the earth."

The book of Acts is about the people of God taking steps to fulfill the command of Acts 1:8. The people of God cross various types of boundaries with the gospel. If one reads Acts with an orientation to God's mission, one finds several important truths. First, this book could easily be called the Acts of the Holy Spirit. Throughout the book, believers give testimony to the work of the Holy Spirit in the mission process. Second, believers cross social and cultural boundaries that have separated them from others, all for the sake of the gospel. It is not an easy process, and often the believers themselves find it difficult to cross those boundaries. But they do it. A third reality is that people take their faith with them throughout the Roman Empire and beyond. Related to this is the purposeful sending of people to take the message of Jesus into new areas. Another important concept is that believers are formed into church communities. People who accept the message become part of the community of believers, those that live out the message of the gospel in the way they live together.

This is not a chapter on the history of Christian mission. But it is important to briefly describe some of the ways Christians have crossed boundaries and barriers of many kinds to take the gospel to others. Dedicated missionaries did this work, but other people on the move also participated in mission as they took their faith with them and shared it with others. Some of the efforts clearly reflect the Jesus Way, while others are clearly contrary to this understanding of mission.

During the first century, the gospel spread throughout the Roman Empire. Tradition also states that Thomas, one of the disciples, made it all the way to India by 52 CE. There was significant persecution at times throughout the Roman Empire, but there were churches in most parts of the empire by the middle of the second century after Christ. This expansion was the work of both formal missionaries and Christians who took their faith with them as they moved throughout the empire. Some of the most important missionaries of those early years were slaves and laborers who moved or were moved as economic opportunities changed throughout the Roman Empire.

The first major conversion outside of the Roman Empire happened in Armenia in 304 CE when Christianity became that kingdom's state religion. By 313 the Roman emperor Constantine legalized Christianity in the empire, ending the persecution of believers and opening the way for Christianity to become the imperial religion by the end of the century. Ethiopia made Christianity its official religion in 330. And this process continued in many countries on the edge of the Roman Empire.

John Driver describes the expansion of the church during these early centuries this way:

> Probably the most important ingredient in the extension of the Church was the reality of a Christian people, different, present in the midst of the empire, whose members offered a vital and dynamic worship and who insisted on talking about their faith and life wherever people would listen. Priscilla and Aquila would be examples of this in the New Testament. But the protagonists of this effort in the 2nd and 3rd centuries have mostly remained anonymous.[2]

In the fifth century, missionaries went to Ireland and bishops were named for Herat (Afghanistan) and Samarkand (Uzbekistan). Also, the first Nestorian missionaries reached China during this century.[3] And this story was repeated in many places as monks and travelers took Christian faith with them along the Silk Road and into most of Europe, northern Africa, the Middle East, and Central Asia. Some of these missionaries saw powerful signs from God that convinced people to become believers.

Even though most people were not literate and the Bible had to be copied by hand, it was translated into new languages as Christian faith moved eastward. Churches aligned with the Roman bishop were adopting Latin as the language of the church, and churches aligned with the bishop in Constantinople were increasingly using Greek. But peoples outside those areas of influence were seeing the Bible translated into some of the major languages of their own regions.

But all was not well with Christian mission. As kings or princes converted, they often forced their subjects to become Christians or imposed certain doctrinal perspectives by force. This move is sometimes called the "Constantinian shift" because of the powerful effects of Emperor Constantine's toleration and then preferential treatment of Christianity in the fourth-century Roman Empire. A faith that had been persecuted was now capable of using political and military force to impose Christian faith and to punish Christians perceived as heretics.

As kings and princes became Christians, they "Christianized" their subjects. There were also cases of peoples being Christianized by conquest. Attempts to invite people into authentic discipleship were completely lost in many of these "massive conversions." Many rebelled against these efforts. State power was used for mission or to defend (and impose) "orthodox" understandings of Christian faith. This created situations where Christian political leaders went to war with each other. War became a tool to defend or impose a certain theological understanding of specific Christian doctrines.

During this Constantinian era, several important events changed the face of Christianity around the Mediterranean. On the one hand, the Prophet Muhammad rose to power in early seventh-century Arabia. He saw Christians fighting each other over doctrine and questioned whether this could be from God. Islam also used the military in its mission expansion. Within decades the "house of Islam" extended from Central Asia to the Atlantic shores of Morocco and the Iberian Peninsula. Christian communities throughout the Middle East and North Africa either converted to Islam or accepted a restricted existence. The fear of Muslim conquest became particularly important in southern Europe and in Orthodox lands. That fear would shape Christian thinking about Islam for several centuries.

From the eleventh century, militant European Christians launched a series of "Crusades" to recapture formerly Christian lands from Muslim control. The focus of the Crusades was usually the Holy Land. But crusaders also fought to retake Spain, conquer Slavic pagans, and persecute other European Christians who had been deemed heretical. In 1204, crusaders even sacked the capital of Eastern Christianity, Constantinople. Christian soldiers murdered Jews and burned synagogues throughout the Crusades.

The other major change during this period was the mutual excommunication of Rome and Constantinople in 1054. This created, arguably, the most significant division in the history of Christianity. Most other expressions of Christian faith found themselves identifying with one side or the other. Smaller Christian expressions continued to exist outside the influence of Rome and Constantinople, particularly in the growing Islamic world or beyond. In the midst of these transformations, Christian congregations in China completely disappeared. It seemed that Christian faith elsewhere might continue to shrink because of the military expansion of Islam.

The complexities of the Christian encounter with Islam can be seen clearly in Iberia. Under Islamic rule, Muslims, Christians, and Jews occasionally collaborated, especially in intellectual and artistic endeavors. Jews, in fact, enjoyed relative freedom under Muslim rule compared to their experience under the previous Christian rulers. But Christians found their new and increasingly onerous restrictions hard to bear. Christian armies slowly won back land over a four-hundred-year period, a process known as the Reconquista ("Reconquest"). The Catholicism that emerged from this period was militantly orthodox. Muslims as well as Jews were forced to convert, but even then, they and their descendants were suspected of harboring heretical or non-Christian beliefs and so were subject to inquisition and torture.

Descendants of the Jews forced out of "reconquered" Spain and Portugal later experienced the horrors of the Holocaust. The more immediate effects of militant Iberian Christianity were felt elsewhere, during the period of imperial mission. Spanish and Portuguese expansion into the Americas, Africa, and parts of Asia brought with it a growth in the number of Catholic missionaries and religious orders that began to evangelize the areas that came under the imperial control of these countries. In many ways it was an evangelization of "the cross and the sword." Very dedicated monks went into the Spanish and Portuguese colonies, taking the Catholic message with them and baptizing many people. Soldiers often accompanied the monks, ready to protect them but also to impose Catholic faith on those who were conquered. Both countries went out assuming that their task of colonization was blessed by God.

It was clearly blessed by the pope, who issued proclamations dividing the "new world" between Spain and Portugal.

Christopher Columbus famously arrived in the Caribbean in 1492, the same year the Spanish Reconquista concluded. Only twenty-five years later, in 1517, Martin Luther published his *Ninety-Five Theses* challenging the theology of merit he saw as underlying the widespread sale of indulgences (certificates of payment to reduce time spent in purgatory). Luther's developing theology of salvation "by grace alone" struck a nerve in Western Christendom. During the ensuing Reformation, partisans of Luther and other Protestant leaders began their own movements. After decades of open conflict, Lutheran, Reformed ("Calvinist"), and Catholic Christians divided Europe among themselves. More "radical" reforming movements, such as the Anabaptists, experienced persecution and marginalization.

All the surviving Christian movements from this period eventually participated to some degree in Western imperialism. In response to Protestantism as well as internal pressures, Catholicism launched an aggressive mission strategy near the end of the sixteenth century. Catholic missionaries traveled throughout the Americas as well as to India, China, and Japan. Protestant mission became a major enterprise with the rise of the British Empire in the eighteenth and nineteenth centuries. Even marginalized European Christians either joined the mainstream mission movement or benefited from imperialism through trade and migration.

The expansion of European imperialism had a devastating effect on much of the world. In the Americas, enslavement and mass murder combined with the (sometimes intentional) spread of European diseases to wipe out almost the entire Indigenous population. Surviving Indigenous communities were displaced and diminished by colonial settlements, not only in the Americas, but also in South Africa, Australia, and New Zealand. The horrors of the Atlantic slave trade were felt in Africa as well as the Americas. Famine caused by British mismanagement in India resulted in up to fifteen million deaths.

Missionaries, Catholic and Protestant, were no doubt often tools of empire, helping to subjugate conquered populations. Even when they sincerely desired the well-being of Indigenous peoples, they rarely questioned their countries' imperial rights. In some areas, though, colonial governments tried to restrict missionary access because they feared the liberating effect of the gospel. Some missionaries showed courage in their struggles for Indigenous rights and in their attempts to preserve and honor Indigenous cultures. Two missionaries to China in particular, Jesuit Matteo Ricci in the sixteenth century and Protestant Hudson Taylor in the nineteenth century, are known for their deep sensitivity to their host culture. Gambian missiologist Lamin Sanneh, moreover, argues that the work of missionaries to translate the Bible into local languages was more than a sign of respect. It also provided tools for Indigenous resistance to imperialism. Sanneh sees this process as a reason for the massive growth of Christianity in post-colonial Africa.[4]

European Christians assumed that God was blessing their mission enterprise and that Christian Europe was superior to the rest of the world. European settler colonial societies, particularly in the United States, adopted this ethos as their own. This ethos explains why evangelization and Americanization have often gone together.

In many ways, the Edinburgh Missionary Conference in 1910 marks the high point and the end of this model of mission. The conference brought together over twelve hundred Protestant leaders, mostly but not exclusively from Europe and

North America. Its confident paternalism was expressed as a grave concern for Indians under British imperial rule, and in the controversial removal of Latin America from the agenda. Latin America, as a Catholic region, was judged not to be a mission field. On the other hand, the conference strengthened a commitment to empowering collaboration with local leaders and ecumenical partners. A long, slow transition toward non-competitive, indigenous-led mission had begun.

Europe's shift to a humbler form of mission was facilitated by the shocks of two world wars—and of widespread Christian complicity in fascism and the Holocaust. The long Cold War that settled in after the Second World War saw the emergence of the United States as the bearer of global Christian leadership, posed against an officially atheistic Soviet Union.

During the Cold War period, the United States developed a new form of imperialism. Rather than conquering new lands and incorporating them into an empire, the United States built military bases around the world[5] and dominated global security partnerships. America, moreover, used its growing financial power to make most foreign governments dependent on its currency, loans, and trade. The global influence of American brands, pop stars, and movies further bolstered America's claim to be the land of the free. American mission often participated in this "neo-imperial" expansion of American economic and cultural power. For instance, American denominations and mission agencies established global outposts, dominated ecumenical partnerships, and made foreign ministries dependent on American money. Although the Cold War ended in the early 1990s, many of these neo-imperial patterns persist.

While the Spanish and Portuguese Empires had fallen apart in the nineteenth century, British, Dutch, Belgian, and other European powers maintained their colonial holdings through

World War II. But in the decades after the war, independence movements throughout Africa and Asia led to the creation of dozens of new states. Decolonization heralded a new era for Christian mission. This era is sometimes described as a shift from the imperial "center" to the postcolonial "periphery." One sign of this shift is the global influence of Latin American and other liberation theologies. Another is the steady arrival of African, Asian, and Latin American missionaries to secularizing Europe and North America.

The face of global Christianity changed rapidly during the twentieth century.[6] At the beginning of the twentieth century, 66 percent of Christians lived in Europe. By 2010, the numbers had shifted radically. By that time, 26 percent of Christians lived in Europe and 74 percent lived in other parts of the world. Also, the number of Christians in the world had gone from about 600 million to more than 2 billion.[7] What accounted for this rapid change?

One can point to several factors that are beyond the scope of this book. But several important issues can be named here. On the one hand, secularization has led to a significant decline of Christian faith in Europe and its settler colonies. The possible exception to this decline is the United States, whose Christian ranks are bolstered by immigrants. On the other hand, Christianity in Africa and Asia has grown enormously. Catholicism has been a major beneficiary of this growth. So have Pentecostal and charismatic movements, which now claim over six hundred million adherents worldwide. The success of Pentecostalism is in part thanks to its malleability. The historic Pentecostal denominations, which trace their roots to the 1906 Azusa Street Revival in Los Angeles, have millions of global members. Millions more belong to an incredible array of independent churches.

The experience of the Orthodox churches has been mixed. Atheist regimes in the Soviet Union, Ethiopia, and elsewhere brought official persecution of Orthodox believers for decades. Their communities have begun to recover since the fall of communism in the early 1990s. The ancient communities of Egypt and the Middle East, however, have experienced new waves of persecution, and many churches are vanishing.

As churches have been involved in mission throughout the centuries, a number of questions and issues have arisen. Many of the most vexing questions have come as a result of Christians having political, economic, and military power. Human power has been seen as an asset to mission. But it has often created profound ethical and moral questions. Because of these issues, many have concluded that Christians should not be involved in mission.

Given these concerns about mission, what are some of the questions we need to address?

Who should do mission? In the book of Acts we already see two types of mission efforts, those done by people who live their lives as followers of Jesus as they move to new locations, and those done by missionaries, people sent out to do mission. As churches became more established and countries became Christianized, the task became more specialized. Since everyone in each Christianized country was considered to be a Christian already, there was no need for people to talk about Jesus with their neighbors. They might still seek to help the poor and needy, but inviting people to faith became something done "out there," in other regions around the world.

Eventually, this tendency drove a wedge between churches and missionaries. Mission was something done by missionaries, be they from Catholic religious orders or later from Protestant mission societies. Those who crossed boundaries with the gospel often did so at great personal risk. Many of those who went out with the gospel suffered martyrdom. The role of the average Christian in Christianized countries became that of praying for and financially supporting missionaries, not actually participating directly in mission.

The New Testament concept of all Christians involved in mission tended to continue in places where Christians were a minority. Those Christians continued to share their faith with those around them.

How is mission related to and influenced by money and power? When Jesus sends out his disciples, he tells them that they will receive power from the Holy Spirit to be his witnesses (Acts 1:8). Throughout the first centuries of the church this was clearly the way Christians thought about the task. Churches sent out formal missionaries, but these missionaries usually traveled with limited resources and with a clear sense that they were dependent on God working through them.

The situation became complex when Christians began to have political, economic, or military power. How was that power to be used? How did it relate to what God was doing? How did money and power influence or distort the mission of the church? How do we make sense of the profound damage or destruction that has been inflicted on people in the name of Christian mission?

A variation on that question was how doing mission from the center affected the way that those on the periphery experienced the message and the methods of mission. If there was a significant cultural or social difference between the missionaries and the people, how might that distort the gospel?

Because much of Western mission over the last five centuries has been done from positions of power, it is difficult for many to think of mission without these resources. This is a particularly complex issue for Christians from the West, who have inherited a model of mission that assumes that mission is done from positions of power and that extensive resources are crucial to successful mission.

How does Christian faith interact with other faiths? The question of other faiths has always been an issue, since the call of the gospel includes an invitation to follow Jesus Christ. When Christian mission was done from a position of "weakness," the invitation was not forced or pressured. The person proclaiming the gospel depended on the work of the Holy Spirit to move people to make a decision.

But the issue of power and competition has been part of the equation throughout most of the modern mission movement. At times people have been forced to become Christians or have been "encouraged" through the offer of resources such as food or access to power. Indigenous peoples have been forced into missions, their children have been taken from them, their lands have been confiscated, all in the name of Christian faith and civilization. Christian missionaries have often entered new areas with the garb of "advanced" societies, and so it has not been clear whether people have accepted the faith of Jesus or the "possibilities" of social advancement.

On the other hand, Christians who live in places where they are minorities are often persecuted for their faith. Today, this is the experience of many Christians in the Middle East, China, and parts of Africa. The lives of Christians in many Muslim countries are often made more difficult by the repercussions of American and European military actions.

Yet minority Christians also find ways to thrive, and their faith can be sharpened through creative interaction with the majority culture. These Christians usually remain committed to sharing the gospel, and doing so without having recourse to state power puts them in a closer situation to that of Jesus and his disciples than that of the imperial missionaries.

Reports of conversions after "power encounters," in which testimony to faith in Christ is accompanied by signs and wonders, are common. When possible, interfaith dialogue offers opportunities for mutual understanding and collaboration, without diminishing the universal call of the gospel. In places where public witness is outlawed, "insider movements" frequently develop through which Christians employ language and customs of the dominant religion to give expression to their faith. Christians in Muslim majority contexts may, for example, describe themselves as followers of Isa (Arabic for Jesus).

By contrast, many Christians in Europe and North America have become wary of sharing their faith at all. Driven by a desire to rectify past and present harms, they declare all religions to be equally true and valid. Although this impulse toward humility and repentance is praiseworthy in many respects, it typically underestimates the intellectual and cultural difficulties of interreligious encounters. As we learn from minority Christians, genuine respect for other religions as well as for one's own faith requires careful listening and transparent witness to salvation in Christ.

What is the scope of Christian mission? As we think about what God is doing in the world and what Christians need to be doing, we face important questions about the scope of our task. As we read the stories in the New Testament, the message often focuses on the call for conversion and transformation of individuals. The testimonies in the Gospels and the book of Acts are about people who encounter Jesus and experience physical, emotional, and spiritual transformation on a personal level. Yet the message of the gospel always points to something bigger. The God of creation is working to heal all of creation from the damage of sin. The end point of the Bible includes ecological and cosmic renewal.

Because the end point is grand and cosmic, it is important to reflect on where Christians and the church fit in that process. This is not at all easy. The "Christian" empires and countries have assumed that they are creating the new society through their efforts. When Constantine became a believer in fourth-century Rome and legalized Christian faith, many people saw that as the beginning of God's kingdom on earth. The kings that extended Christian faith by the sword assumed that they were creating "Christian" societies. And although we should rightly reject efforts to do God's work by violent human power, all of these efforts focused on something bigger than individual transformation. They thought that they could transform societies and nations.

Throughout the history of the church, an alternative to this form of mission can be seen in efforts to form voluntary communities of Christians committed to being salt and light in the midst of a world that will not reach perfection until the eschaton, when God acts definitively to redeem all things. The monastic movement represented this alternative during the period of Western Christendom, though it also became deeply involved in European imperialism. Similar movements that were more skeptical of imperial violence—for instance, the Anabaptists during the Reformation—were deemed heretical and persecuted by the majority church. The tremendous growth of independent Pentecostal churches today may be partly explained by this impulse toward noncoercive communities of faith whose witness emerges from the quality of their care for one another (see John 13:35). Although the eschatological bent of these communities can lead them in unhealthy directions, it can also free them to trust God for the fate of nations and focus on practical discipleship within their context.

In the midst of all of what we have described, Christian faith continues to expand, particularly from the peripheries to the secularized centers of power. The "average" Christian today does not look like a Christian from the West. She probably is under age twenty, is a young mother, has limited formal educa-tion, is a charismatic Catholic or Pentecostal, and is from the Philippines, Brazil, or a country in sub-Saharan Africa. One of the key challenges for Christians from the West is whether we can recognize this young woman as our sister in Christ and whether we can accept her as our equal before Christ. Because our forms of Christian faith have seemed normative for so long and because we are in positions of relative power, it will be tempting to ignore or belittle her. But we will be most fully in a Jesus Way mode of mission when we recognize that our sister looks more like the average Christian than we do and that she is at the cutting edge of God's mission in the world.

3

Church as Missional Community

You are the salt of the earth; but if salt has lost its taste, how can its saltiness be restored? It is no longer good for anything, but is thrown out and trampled under foot.

You are the light of the world. A city built on a hill cannot be hid. No one after lighting a lamp puts it under the bushel basket, but on the lampstand, and it gives light to all in the house. In the same way, let your light shine before others, so that they may see your good works and give glory to your Father in heaven.
—Matthew 5:13-16

Rosa del Carmen Ortez-Cruz fled domestic violence in her native Honduras in 2002. She made it to Greensboro, North Carolina, where she was able to establish a more peaceful life with her children. But in 2018, as the Trump administration increased pressure on undocumented immigrants throughout the United States, Ortez-Cruz received a deportation order from Immigration and Customs Enforcement. She got in touch with a local Mennonite pastor, Isaac Villegas, and took sanctuary in the Church of the Reconciliation, the Presbyterian church that shared its space with Villegas's Chapel Hill Mennonite Fellowship.

As Ortez-Cruz waited and hoped within the church's walls, she was accompanied by members of the Mennonite and Presbyterian churches who saw their work as an extension of God's love and as a response to God's call to welcome strangers. After Ortez-Cruz had spent two years in sanctuary, legal advocates were able to overturn the deportation order and she returned home to live with her children.

In common parlance, we say that the church has a mission. But if we take the Bible seriously, we need to remember that it is not that the church has a mission, but that God's mission has a church. God is at work in the world, and God invites us to be a part of the task. We cannot understand what the church is about unless we understand that it is part of what God is doing in the world.

We stated earlier that Jesus Way mission cannot be reduced to one aspect of what Jesus did on earth. In the same way, if we want to understand what the church in mission is about, we need to look beyond the passages where Jesus commands his disciples to continue his task on earth. Jesus used many images to describe what the church was supposed to look like and what it was supposed to do in the world. And the New Testament draws on many metaphors to describe what the church is about. This wide variety of images goes well beyond verbal proclamation and invitation to accept Jesus. In *Images of the Church in Mission*, John Driver organizes the biblical images that describe what the followers of Jesus are to do and how they are to be in the world into four broad categories of pilgrimage, new order, peoplehood, and transformation.[1] God's work in the world through the church is so broad and diverse that no one image can adequately summarize the church's mission in the world. God's mission is at the core of what it means to be a community of believers in Jesus Christ.

At several points in the New Testament, the followers of Jesus are called pilgrims, or sojourners, people on the move (Hebrews 11:13; 1 Peter 2:11). We are called, like Abraham, to go to the land of promise, to be a blessing to all the peoples of the earth (Genesis 12; Hebrews 11). This image points to the recognition that "this world is not my home," that we are citizens of God's kingdom (Philippians 3:20; Ephesians 2:19). But it also points to the fact that we are people of the Way (as described in Acts 9:2; 24:14, 22), those who follow in the way of Jesus. Jesus chose the way of the cross, and believers are part of God's mission when they follow the way of the cross, dedicating their lives to healing and liberation even in the face of opposition. Another important aspect of this series of images is the concept of the poor. It is the poor who are blessed and the poor to whom we are to preach the good news of the gospel (Luke 4:18; 6:20). The poor are the special objects of God's mission.

Believers are also part of God's new order that is developing on earth. As citizens of the kingdom, we live today in light of God's future. We invite others to live into the future today. We also seek manifestations of the future, through changed lives, miracles, and other signs that point us toward the day when there will be no brokenness, illness, or death. Because we are part of God's new creation, God's new humanity, we are signs and sacraments of that future. Our task is to point people toward that future and to be the means through which the Spirit of God can manifest that future in the lives of others.

The images related to peoplehood point to what God is creating and the type of relationship God wants with humans. These images have deep roots in the Old Testament where God calls Abraham to form a people with whom God will form a covenant relationship (Genesis 12). Humans often violate that relationship, but God keeps at the task. God also wants us to be a family, to demonstrate the links and commitments to each other that demonstrate that we see each other as siblings (John 13:34-35; Ephesians 2:11-22). Jesus also compares us to sheep in a metaphor in which he is the good shepherd who deeply cares for his sheep and will do anything needed to take care of them (Matthew 18:10-14; Luke 15:1-7).

The images of transformation point to the importance of our public testimony and practice in God's mission. The previous images focus on what God is doing and how we are to live. These images point to the task of giving witness to what God is doing through word and deed. In Matthew 5, Jesus calls us to be salt, light, and a city on a hill. We are to serve our world by having a positive influence, by providing direction, and by giving an example. Paul and Peter talk about Christians as living stones who are part of God's living temple (1 Corinthians 3:16-17; 1 Peter 2:4-5). All of these images point to the reality that the community of believers is to be a community of witnesses who give testimony to what God has done, is doing, and will do in the future.

If mission is understood in this broad way, it means that everything the church does should have a mission orientation, even though not all its actions will be directly missional. The Jesus Way perspective on mission is that the church, as a local worshiping community of believers, is to live out its faith in such a way that it fulfills its mission. In *Building on the Rock*, author Walfred Fahrer posits that a faithful Jesus Way church will be a missional church.

> We are closer to Jesus' vision of church when we see it as a faith community whose value system is shaped by the life and teachings of Jesus and whose relationships are characterized by a strong, loving commitment. . . .
>
> We are closer to the vision of Christ for the church when inviting others to faith is not just the task of the faith community, but its very identity. The message of the gospel we communicate is not simply about getting to heaven but about getting heaven to earth.[2]

In his book, Fahrer describes what it means to be a church together as we build on who Jesus is, what he did, and what he calls us to. The author builds a model of a primary alternative community where the life of the local congregation is closely linked to its witness and mission to the world. As we link together how we disciple new believers (*deliberate discipleship*), how we understand the authority of Scripture and of leaders in the congregation (*an alternative vision of authority*), and the way we understand spirituality (*a specific spirituality of nonviolent love*), we develop communities of *intentional invitation* where mission is a natural part of who we are and how we understand our reason for existence in the world.[3]

This Jesus Way of mission focuses on believers and local congregations as the place where mission begins and is best expressed. Being a church in mission is about being active witnesses, through confession and life, of what God has done in us and about God's invitation to live in the way of Jesus. It recognizes that fundamentally this is about what God is doing through the Spirit in us and in our world.

We invite others to the way of Jesus by how we live, how we follow Jesus' teaching together, how we love God and others, but also through an intentional yet natural invitation. Our mission is to be the presence of Jesus, to witness to the work of God in the world, to live together in the power of the Holy Spirit, to serve the world, to be agents of God's reconciliation and transformation, and to invite others to join us in the Jesus Way.

This has implications for how we do mission in the world. The New Testament describes us as light and salt, as the presence of Jesus, and by many other images that encourage us in our local role as testimonies to those around us.

Yet we also have a larger role. Jesus sent his disciples out into the world, so our mission includes the development of communities and the growth of believers in various parts of the world. This dimension of our mission is the subject of the next chapter.

SIGNS AND SACRAMENTS

The South African missiologist David Bosch stated that the church is to live into God's future today. He called on churches to be signs and sacraments of what God is doing in the world and God's future for humanity.[4] This call reminds us that the church exists for others, for the world around it. We are signs pointing to what God is doing and we are the sacraments, the means of grace, so that God's work in the world may be made visible.

As we live into God's future, we give testimony of what God is doing on the earth and what God's future for humanity looks like. As we live as a community of faith, we point to how God wants humans to live together. As we pray for the sick, we point to that day when there will be no more sickness.

As we seek to repair the injustices of racism and colonialism, we point to that day when all people will be reconciled in Christ. As we help each other, we point toward the day when there will be no more need. As we allow the Spirit of God to move us and help us grow, we become signs of what God is doing through Jesus Christ, in the power of the Holy Spirit. When we follow the Spirit and go into the world preaching the Word of Jesus Christ, we continue Jesus' work in the world, giving testimony (signs) to the reality of what God is doing for our world.

And as we go into the world as testimonies of what Jesus did, in the power of the Spirit, we become the means, or sacrament, that God uses to give grace to the world. God works through us to touch the world. As signs and sacraments, we do not confuse our sinful, broken attempts at missional community with the fullness of God's presence. Instead, we discern and follow God's call humbly and celebrate when others see Christ in us.

4

Incarnational Mission

I have become all things to all people, so that I might by any means save some.
   —1 Corinthians 9:22 (NRSVA)

In the late sixteenth century, Italian Jesuit missionary Matteo Ricci and his colleagues became convinced that the only way the gospel would gain a hearing in China was by taking an authentically Chinese form. Mindful that Jesuits in the Americas were participating in the destruction of Indigenous cultures, these missionaries sought to honor their host culture by adopting the dress and customs of respected Confucian court philosophers. By carefully studying Chinese language, history, and culture, and by training converts—men as well as women[1]—to become church leaders, they hoped to foster a Chinese version of Christianity under the direction of Chinese leadership.

Three hundred years later, a young English Methodist, Hudson Taylor, sensed a divine call to join the mission in China. He, too, thought the gospel would take root on Chinese soil only if missionaries were willing to affirm the culture of the people they were seeking to reach. He argued, from the example of the apostle Paul, "Let us in everything not sinful become like the Chinese, that by all means we may 'save some.'"[2] Taylor's organization, China Inland Mission, required its missionaries to take on Chinese dress and customs, and to journey into the country's interior, far from the detached compounds where most Protestant missionaries lived.

Part of our incarnational confession is that the gospel can be faithfully lived out in any culture and in any language. Christian missionaries have worked to translate the Bible, or portions of it, into most of the languages of the earth. As new believers develop churches, these communities of faith develop within the cultural and linguistic idiom of those people. It is not that human cultures are perfect. Rather, all cultures are part of God's good creation and so, despite their limitations, can bear witness to the gospel. Because humans both reflect the fact that we are God's creation and are harmed by sin, our cultures, and our churches, also reflect both. The gospel will challenge all cultures, but can also be lived out (incompletely) in all cultures. Of course, this also means that there is no Christian culture or Christian nation. Also, there are no human systems that are "better vehicles" for living out the way of Jesus. (This last statement is particularly difficult for people from traditionally "Christian" cultures to accept, since we tend to use Christian as an adjective and not merely as a noun. We are convinced that some cultures are more "Christian" than others.)

Jesus Christ became a human; he incarnated himself into a specific human culture, at a specific time in its history. He lived out God's work for humanity within a specific environment.

Jesus also called his followers to continue his mission in the same way. What does it look like in practice to say that the incarnation is our model for mission in the world?

MISSION AS INCARNATIONAL BRIDGE

To believe in the incarnation is to confess that the distances between cultures can ultimately be surmounted, that we are not condemned to isolation from one another. But it also means following the model of Jesus, who incarnated himself by becoming human. This means that I, as a follower of Christ, am to be the bridge, to seek to become Jesus to the other. That is why the missionary strategy of Taylor and the Jesuits was so crucial. It is my responsibility to reach out and "in everything not sinful [to] become like the Chinese." Throughout the centuries, Christian missionaries have chosen to live among other people, learn their languages, and learn to live like them. This is how they then have been able to talk about Jesus in ways that connect and make sense to people in the host culture.

A corollary of this understanding has been the importance given to translating the Bible into the languages of the world. And related to this have been the literacy programs that have taught people to read their own languages. If the gospel can be incarnated into any human culture, it can also be expressed in any human language. Many missionaries have given their lives to learn the language of a small people group and then to translate the Bible into their language.

Henry Venn, a U.S. mission leader during the nineteenth century, developed the three-self concept. He postulated that a church was effectively established in a specific culture when it was self-governing, self-supporting, and self-propagating.[3] This was a particularly crucial challenge to the colonial era of mission, where control, finances, and mission often stayed in the hands of the missionaries for a long time. If the gospel had been incarnated in the new host culture, then it would produce a church that would now continue the task of mission on its own, within its own culture and people. As churches became global during the twentieth century, it became clear that they also needed to be self-theologizing and self-defining in relationship to cultural models of organization, worship, and community life.[4] These became important markers in the life and development of churches in various cultures around the world.[5]

Of course, these ways of thinking about the church within a cultural framework look different in the age of globalization. What does that three-self concept look like when globalization blurs the lines between cultures? Considering this and similar questions may lead to a more relational and collaborative understanding of the need for missionaries to engage their host cultures.

The incarnational model raises several important questions in practice. On the one hand, all of us are culturally defined. We all were born into and framed by our own culture. And we all tend to think that ours is the "best" culture. In Christian circles, we often assume that the most faithful expression of Christian faith is the one that formed us. Again, this problem is particularly pressing when faith is equated with power, such as in the white nationalism that is once more gaining traction in Europe and North America. So it becomes complicated to actually live into an incarnational model of ministry. Unsurprisingly, some missionaries have been quick to condemn any practice that does not fit into the way they are used to expressing their faith.

But the opposite can also become a problem. The well-meaning attempt to show respect for other cultures can lead to an unwillingness to say anything critical about them. In this way we can lose our sense of how the gospel challenges all cultures, including but not only our own. Incarnational missionaries live in this tension between adaptation and confrontation. They are always faced with the questions, "What is the gospel, and what is (merely) cultural? What is sin, and what is just different from our experience?" Asking these questions can open up healthy questioning of their own faith and culture.

These questions about incarnational mission are important regardless of whether we are reaching out to our neighbors or moving to a new culture. As the stories of Taylor and the Jesuits show, there is great value in having dedicated missionaries who are ready to cross cultural bridges and become incarnated in other cultures. But this is also the task of all followers of Christ. We work to be in the midst of the situation of others, to understand and care for them deeply, to live alongside them and love them as our neighbors.

Incarnation is about connecting with others in their spaces. The Spirit calls us to cross social and cultural barriers so that we might be the presence of Christ to and with others. This means adapting to them and their ways. We learn their language, their customs, and their ways of understanding. We carefully discern, through respectful engagement and listening, what God is doing in their midst. As we preach and practice the gospel of healing and liberation among them, we walk the Jesus Way.

SERVANTS WHO GIVE THEIR LIVES FOR OTHERS

Incarnation is about the way of Jesus. He came to serve, not to be served. In John 13 we find Jesus taking up a common practice within his culture, footwashing, to teach his followers this lesson. They were scandalized that he, their leader, wanted to wash their feet, but he insisted and told them he did so as an example to them.

If footwashing is a model of how God wants us to be in relationship to those around us, then it is clear that Christians are to take up roles as servants within the cultures where we are called to minister. We are meant not to seek power and privilege, but rather to spend our lives for the benefit of others.

Understanding mission as service means addressing immediate felt needs. One of the key issues of incarnational mission is that we seek to serve the other, beginning from where they perceive their initial need. Connection happens at the point of immediate need—whether that need is related to health, disaster, emotional pain, financial crisis, relational issues, or other concerns. They define the situation and need, first. The gospel goes deeper and must address the issues people may not be able to name, such as how sin is manifested in their own culture. But the gospel begins to reach them by connecting with their immediate needs.

From this perspective, incarnational mission not only involves inviting people into the way of Jesus as we live and proclaim the message. It also means that when we invite people to accept the message, we invite them to make it their own, to live it out in their own culture and environment. In other words, we invite people to show in their own lives how Jesus meets the immediate and the deepest needs of their cultures. We invite them to become incarnational missionaries, too.

There is a paradox here worth thinking about. Serving others means empowering them, helping them meet their material and spiritual needs so that they in turn might serve others. The ultimate goal is not service—having less and less, abasing oneself before others—but rather abundant life for all. Service is necessary to reach abundance because of the sin and violence that harm our world. We serve by struggling alongside those most affected by those forces.

Sometimes this paradox is lost, and Christian language of "service" is used to tell people who don't have much and people in pain that they should just accept their lot in life, because God calls them to be servants. Poor people and enslaved people, women and children suffering abuse, and others have thus been told that God wills their suffering.

But service in the Jesus Way of mission directly challenges this distortion of the servanthood message. Jesus served to empower others, to nurture an abundant life for all. Powerful forces opposed his mission and made him suffer for it. Following Jesus into empowering servanthood risks this same opposition—it does not sanction the forces that cause suffering.

WHAT DOES INCARNATIONAL MISSION LOOK LIKE?

Some recent examples of mission in the Jesus Way can help us understand what incarnational mission looks like. At the beginning of chapter 1, we spoke of how the Servant Partners organization took up John Perkins's invitation and model by sending missionaries to live in poor urban communities. These missionaries gather groups of people to study the Bible and worship Jesus, and at the same time, they work to empower local leaders to address structural injustices and start businesses that contribute to community growth.

ReconciliAsian, also based in the Los Angeles area, is another organization dedicated to mission in the Jesus Way. Founders Sue Park-Hur and Hyun Hur were both born in Korea and later migrated to the United States. Their organization seeks to resource Korean immigrant churches with the understanding that reconciliation is at the heart of the gospel—and that this means reconciliation within a politically and generationally fractured Korean community, as well as with other Asian communities. From this base within Asian American churches, ReconciliAsian also spreads the gospel of peace to the divided Korean Peninsula.

Another organization, Christian Peacemaker Teams (CPT), seeks to accompany local peacemakers in conflict zones around the world. With teams in Colombia, Iraqi Kurdistan, Palestine, and the refugee camps on the Greek island of Lesvos, CPT contributes to peace and reconciliation by drawing global attention to the realities of conflict and the local efforts to resist injustice and violence peacefully.

Many more examples could be given: of churches like the ones mentioned in chapter 3 that provide sanctuary for undocumented immigrants; of women and men who see their businesses as callings from God to empower the poor; of Muslims who discreetly share of their faith in Isa al-Masih ("Jesus the Messiah") with their fellow Muslims; of Christians who witness to the gospel through respectful dialogue with members of other religions; of organizations that work at local, regional, and international levels to transform conflicts and challenge injustices in the name of Jesus.

The gospel addresses the difficult issues of the differences between peoples and the competition between us. It calls us to be peacemakers, to seek reconciliation at all levels. It calls us to what René Padilla and other Latin American missiologists have called a "misión integral," an integral or holistic mission.[6] An integral mission means addressing interpersonal problems as well as making structural changes in society. We do all of these things as witness to the gospel, and work at them among believers and nonbelievers.

KEEPING WORD AND DEED TOGETHER

In the Jesus Way of mission there has to be a clear alignment between our actions and our words. We are always tempted to separate these. We may use strong words but fail to act on them. Or we may act boldly but systematically avoid offering an interpretation of our actions that points to their motivation and meaning in the gospel.

The word must create a profound transforming deed through the power of the Holy Spirit; our good deeds, if they are to be mission in the way of Jesus, must have a clear gospel interpretation. We have often created unhelpful divisions between the two. But these divisions are artificial and have contributed greatly to the horrific history of imperial mission that we reviewed in chapter 2—mission in which words about Jesus were divorced from Jesus-like actions.

As the incarnate Word of God, Jesus himself embodies the unity of word and action. Word and deed are, of course, inseparable in all human cultures. But in Jesus, words and actions not only are tied together as a matter of fact, but fulfill their God-given purpose by bearing witness, together, to the integrity and abundance of life with God—the life Hebrew writers described with the term *shalom*, which encompasses peace with God, with other humans, and with all of creation.

We join Jesus' incarnational mission by seeking shalom in all human cultures, respecting those cultures by communicating the gospel in their own terms, empowering leaders from within them, serving their poor and marginalized members, and partnering with them to transform their conflicts.

5

Issues in Mission

But seek the welfare of the city where I have sent you into exile, and pray to the LORD on its behalf, for in its welfare you will find your welfare.
   —Jeremiah 29:7

Part of Hudson Taylor's call for Western missionaries to take their host cultures seriously was that missionaries keep their children with them rather than send them to Europe or North America for education. This controversial move was seen as dangerous at the time, and can be seen as an important step toward incarnational mission. Over time, however, many schools for missionary children developed as outposts of Western culture and language. Missionaries took their children out of their ministry contexts and put them into largely white enclaves, thus sending a clear message about their low regard for the host cultures.

A related dynamic can occur when wealthy and middle-class Christians embrace an incarnational mission of relocating to poor neighborhoods. If they do not think carefully about the economic, political, and cultural issues involved in relocation, they can end up contributing to gentrification—to driving up rents and dislocating the people they came to serve.

As we have seen at various points throughout this book, mission often creates complications. Since it is humans who are involved in mission, there is always tension between our lofty goals and the realities "on the ground." We want to reflect on some of the key issues related to mission so that we can be better prepared to be the people of God in mission.

Some of the issues we address in this chapter have to do with our human fallibility. Because we are sinners, we will always fall short of full faithfulness to the call of Jesus Christ (Romans 3:23). The Holy Spirit empowers and guides us, so God's mission continues. But we have to be constantly attentive to those times and efforts where we are tempted to use human power to attempt to do the work of the Holy Spirit or where our culture and our biases get confused with the message of the gospel. The Jesus Way of mission recognizes that all our efforts will be partial and that the Spirit works in the midst of our weaknesses and frailties.

We also face the fact that some of the complications we encounter are because we live in an increasingly complex world. We are addressing issues and encounters that would have been completely unknown in previous generations. Because we are facing adaptive challenges, we need to be particularly attentive to how the Spirit is working in the world today, so that we join what God is doing and how God is working.

Some Christians conclude that because of the complexities, we should not be involved in mission. Our goal in this chapter is to name the complexities, but also to recognize that mission is God's work and God's call to those of us who want to walk in the Jesus Way. That is why we have to name and address these issues as we seek to be faithful to God's work in the world.

Many Western Christians today are afraid to talk about a unique message and the truth of Jesus in a setting in which we are taught to value difference and the uniqueness of individual perspectives and beliefs. In our desire to be respectful, we may find it difficult to confess the unique role of Jesus in God's work in the world. As we encounter people of other faiths or no faith, we may find that they are good people and we may feel that the gospel has nothing to offer them. As we see the mistakes of our fellow believers in presenting Christian faith in hurtful ways or linking the message to specific political or cultural understandings, we may question whether we want to be identified with a faith that looks "like that." As a result, we often lose the ability to talk about Jesus and may even begin to doubt our own faith. At times we become so unsure that we cannot even talk to our children about our faith in ways that communicate clearly what we believe.

It is helpful to remember that "mission" names, in the first place, what God is doing in the world. The church's purpose, or mission, is to join God. That means we can't refuse to engage in mission—if we are to be the church, we are engaged in mission. But we must think carefully about how we do mission, how our mission looks like God's mission, as that is revealed most fully in Jesus. When we think about the complications of mission, we should keep in mind both that we do have a mission and that our mission can go wrong.

One frequent complication that arises in mission has to do with the diversity of cultures. What works, what faithfully bears witness to the gospel, in one time and place may not work in another. This problem leads some to embrace (or fear) cultural relativism, especially as our cultures change more and more rapidly. But the incarnation points us to how the gospel always takes particular cultural forms. Mission always involves learning about and from different cultures; it is always intercultural.

Committing to an incarnational, intercultural mission does not mean we can ever simply throw off our own culture. Genuine intercultural mission includes an embrace of our own culture, even an "evangelization" of our own culture as we see more clearly how it has enabled witness to the gospel and also how it has fallen short of the gospel. This process often means we have to face the ethnocentrism and other limitations of our own culture or cultures, limitations that distort mission in the Jesus Way.

Mission at its heart involves interpersonal relationships, and all interpersonal relationships are vulnerable to hurt and abuse. It is inevitable that missionaries will sometimes hurt those whom they seek to serve. When this happens, missionaries who take the Jesus Way seriously will repent and make restitution. It can be tempting for missionaries (and their sending churches) to take refuge in their good intentions or to preemptively demand forgiveness from those who have been hurt. Jesus' call to repentance, however, places the burden on—and provides the empowering grace for—the offender to initiate reconciliation (Matthew 5:23-24). Sending churches and mission agencies also need to be honest about the nature and extent of the harm, and to restrict or terminate the missionaries' access if necessary.

When cross-cultural missionaries come from a culture with relatively more power and prestige than the culture they have relocated to, interpersonal hurts can take on a new complexity. Even without such harms, power differences create serious complications within mission. Differences in wealth, education, citizenship, age, race, gender, and other factors can easily distort relationships formed in the context of mission. The history of interactions between cultures and nations also factors in, especially the history of Christian imperialism that we discussed in chapter 2.

Throughout the history of the church, particularly after the Constantinian synthesis of empire and Christian faith, Christians have found themselves needing to ask questions about how power and money impact Christian mission. Clearly, Christians have mistaken and misused human resources. People have been forced to convert or have been punished for believing the "wrong" doctrine. Non-Christians have been forced out of their homes and countries. And countries that call themselves Christian have done many destructive things in the name of Christianity, including conquest, exploitation, and war.

Christian missionaries have also used power and financial resources in ways that have perverted the message they were proclaiming. During the colonial period, missionaries often had the direct protection or at least the indirect support of the colonial powers. Rich missionaries often went into poor areas and confused the gospel message with Western capitalism. Becoming a Christian in these settings often meant having some access to the benefits of the West. To this day, in many settings, Western worship music and styles impose themselves in the global marketplace and the gospel is not **contextualized**.

Missiologist Jonathan Bonk's book *Missions and Money* explores many of these issues, and names some of the ways missionaries seek to avoid facing them: by relating only to

people with similar levels of power, by taking on a lifestyle
that superficially matches that of their host culture, or by
ignoring the ethical issues and celebrating the advantages of
a well-resourced mission.[1] Bonk's own commitment to Jesus
leads him to argue that Jesus' challenging statements about
wealth and power apply to privileged missionaries. Missionaries in the Jesus Way must be ready to give up their privilege,
and when that is impossible, to use it to empower those whom
they are serving.

In a time when many missionaries are migrants and refugees
from the global "periphery" to the global "center," Jeremiah's
letter to his fellow Israelites exiled in Babylon becomes increasingly relevant. God's word to the exiles, according to Jeremiah,
was that they, while being wary of deceptive teaching, should
build homes, plant gardens, start families, and "seek the peace
of the city" in which they were exiled (Jeremiah 29:4-9). God
promises to look after their well-being as they participate in
the well-being of their host culture and maintain their faith.
Missionaries from privileged backgrounds can also learn from
this call to "seek the peace of the city" while embracing their
host cultures, though they will have to be cautious about the
power they bring with them.

Jesus, too, calls us to make peace and even to love our enemies (Matthew 5:44). What does this look like in real life? It
can, if the Jeremiah passage is our guide, look like the ordi-
nary work of faithful living within another culture—though
we know that this in itself is a difficult task requiring close
attention to issues of economics, politics, and culture.

Since the Edinburgh 1910 conference, Christians around
the world have increasingly collaborated in their mission and
witness. But this collaboration was immediately challenged by
two world wars, wars in which supposedly Christian nations

attacked one another. Later in the twentieth century, the United States supported and stirred up civil wars throughout the largely Catholic countries of Latin America.

It was in this context that Mennonite Central Committee released a poster featuring two people hugging each other and the words "A Modest Proposal for Peace: Let the Christians of the World Agree that They Will Not Kill Each Other." This "Modest Proposal" remains sadly relevant as we become more aware of the effects of ongoing American warfare in the Middle East on ancient Christian communities, or as we look at recent conflicts between Russia and Ukraine. It also speaks to the situation in the United States in which police officers, many of them Christians, regularly kill Black and Latino people, many of whom are also Christian.

A commitment to not killing each other would be a minimum step toward fulfilling Jesus' hope that we Christians would be known by our love for one another (John 13:35). Of course, Jesus taught us not to kill anyone, not just to avoid killing fellow Christians. But many Christians remain trapped in what theologian Walter Wink called the "myth of redemptive violence," the idea that our peace and happiness can be secured only through a violent defeat of whatever and whomever we fear as a threat.[2] Ignoring Jesus, as well as Paul's counsel to "never avenge yourselves" (Romans 12:19), we descend into a never-ending spiral of violence.

As the West becomes more secularized, we hear a message of fear from many Christians. Because Christianity has had a privileged position in many countries for many years, the changes feel like persecution. Although some efforts to restrict religious liberty should be taken seriously, Christians—especially white evangelical Christians—retain an enormous amount of power. Many of these Christians find themselves creating alliances that promise to keep them in power, even if it means joining with people and parties that are working in ways that clearly are not in the Jesus Way.

Some of the fear felt by Christians has to do with emerging ethical challenges, for example, around human sexuality, climate change, and artificial intelligence. If some Christians respond defensively in fear to these challenges, others ignore or downplay them. Christians today, as in every era, are called to reexamine our faith in light of the pressing issues of our time. We can neither take refuge in an imagined past nor accept uncritically all claims of progress. We have to do the hard work of discerning what it means to walk in the Jesus Way here and now.

While Christians have lived in privilege in some places, Christians elsewhere have been persecuted for their faith. More Christians were killed for their faith in the twentieth century than at any other time in history. Since the fall of the Soviet Union, much of that persecution has taken place in Islamic countries. The relationship with Islam and other dominant religions is, for Christians in many parts of the world, the most significant issue they face.

Some countries, mostly Islamic ones but also officially atheistic China, restrict the presence of Christianity severely and outlaw mission work. Christian missionaries have spread the gospel in these countries by entering them on other pretenses and smuggling in Bibles and other teaching material. This work has undoubtedly contributed to the formation of authentic Christian communities, even as it can also serve the aims of Western countries looking to open up "closed" countries for their own economic benefit.

These complications arise not only in Western-initiated mission efforts. The Back to Jerusalem movement, for example, has roots in mid-twentieth-century Chinese Christian attempts to evangelize Central Asian Muslims. The movement became a major force in the 1990s, drawing significant Western funding to support its vision of China's role in fulfilling the great commission. If Chinese Christians benefited from the gospel originally going forth from Jerusalem, they now have the God-ordained task of taking it "back" to Jerusalem, that is, of converting Muslims and "unreached people groups" west of China. In this movement, a persecuted church fluidly combines missionary zeal, Chinese nationalism, and Western financial backing.[3]

The Back to Jerusalem movement represents only one face of a larger shift in mission. The World Council of Churches increasingly speaks of "mission from the margins"—of the transformative witness of struggling marginalized communities—and one mission scholar writes of "the gospel from everywhere to everyone."[4] Churches from Africa, Asia, and Latin America are increasingly sending missionaries within and across their regions, as well as to Europe and North America. These missionaries face the normal range of intercultural and interpersonal challenges, as well as issues related to, on the one hand, the experience of racism and anti-immigrant sentiment and, on the other hand, temptations of wealth and power when and where those are available.

The challenges facing the world today are more intensely interconnected than ever. In recognition of this reality, it has become common to talk about how different social structures, identities, and other forms of power intersect with one another to create particular experiences of the world. Theorists of "intersectionality" discuss how multiple components of a person's or community's identity—for example, race, gender, sexuality, class, citizenship, religion—work together to shape their experience of oppression or privilege or both in a given society.[5] This insight can be extended to talk about how we are related to the environment in a time of climate change—Who pollutes, and who suffers the consequences?

As we write this chapter, the world has undergone a series of shocks related to the COVID-19 pandemic. Evidence indicates that the virus was first passed from animals to humans, in a transmission process that is becoming increasingly common as more and more wild animal habitats are destroyed by industry, urban growth, and climate change.

In response to the global spread of the virus, most nations have adopted some form of quarantine, in which people are required to stay home from work and public spaces. Quarantine has had a severe impact on the global economy, but its effects are felt very differently by different people and communities. While the billionaire owners of online retail stores have made more money than ever, the majority of the world's population has struggled to find the resources to pay rent and purchase food and medical care.

These problems are especially visible in countries with weak social safety nets and large informal economies. If, for example, you make your living by cooking and selling food from an unregistered street cart, it is unlikely that you will have any way to cover your bills during quarantine. This makes it more likely that you will break quarantine to make money, and thus more likely that you will get sick—but how will you get medical care?

If you are a woman, your experience may be even more difficult. Women working in the informal economy are the most susceptible to extreme poverty and exploitation, and are often responsible for their families' medical and education needs. During quarantine, women in abusive relationships and children in abusive households often have few options but to stay at home with their abusers.

This is the situation facing billions of people around the world today. A version of this story is also playing out in economically "advanced" countries like the United States. The experience of COVID-19 and quarantine may have contributed to the intensity of the Black Lives Matter protests against the murders of George Floyd, Breonna Taylor, and other Black people by police officers. The coronavirus, like the police, has killed a disproportionate number of Black Americans, as well as Latinos. The economics of quarantine also have a disproportionally negative effect on Black and Latino Americans. These effects are the health and economic outcomes of centuries of racial violence, from slavery to segregation to today's system of mass incarceration.

Reflecting on these realities gives us a sobering awareness of the complexities of Christian mission today. First of all, it is clear that a given congregation's sense of its mission will depend to an important extent on its social and geographical location. Your sense of what God is doing and how you are called to participate will likely vary if members of your church community have been persecuted as ethnic or religious minorities—or not; if members of your church community have contracted and suffered or died from COVID-19—or not; if members of your church community have migrated across international borders to escape poverty—or not. For any church, for any Christian, reaching a clear sense of God's call requires listening to the hopes and needs of our most vulnerable siblings.

The fact that some Christians, and some people and communities more generally, are more vulnerable than others to disease, poverty, police violence, forced migration, and other problems requires a commitment not only to solidarity within the body of Christ, but also to collaborative action around the many intersecting issues that make so many people—and the earth itself—vulnerable to suffering and devastation. The way of incarnational solidarity, the Jesus Way of healing and liberation, is more relevant than ever.

Other issues are likely to arise where Christians will struggle with what it means to be faithful to God's mission in the world. And Christians will continue to confuse human power with the Spirit's work. Sin will also have an impact on the best intentions of sincere people. But as we seek to be faithful to the call of the gospel, we would do well to consciously orient our understanding and practice of mission to the Jesus Way.

We have mentioned all of these aspects at various points in the book. But it is helpful to list them together as a way of recognizing what we mean by a Jesus Way of doing mission.

Letting go of power in expectation of God's powerful work. As followers of Jesus Christ, we need to constantly remember that our mission is done in the power of the Holy Spirit. We are messengers and servants, but the work is God's. This is an invitation to both humility and expectation. But it is also a recognition that God uses "loaves and fishes" and praises the extravagant gift of the poor widow.

Being attentive to the peripheries. Because God invites us to humility and expectation, we are also invited to recognize that God often works from the peripheries. Today, immigrants from many parts of the Global South are becoming missionaries to the more secular North. We are invited to recognize God at work through them. We are also invited to recognize the presence of Jesus in the poor and marginalized.

Witnessing through word and deed. We will be closest to God's mission when our lives are involved in serving others, when our churches live as communities of faith, and when we explain what our witness means. Integrity of word and deed is essential for incarnational mission.

Serving as agents of peacemaking and reconciliation. We are called to seek the peace of the city, to join in God's movement of shalom. Since God is active in reconciling enemies, transforming conflicts, and resisting injustice, we should be too.

Living into love in a world of fear. The rapid changes in our world lead some Christians to take a fearful, defensive stance. But God's "perfect love casts out fear" (1 John 4:18), enabling us to participate confidently and humbly in God's mission. Our witness is attractive when our lives have been liberated by God's love into love for others.

Engaging in interreligious dialogue and the witness to the gospel. Love for others means listening to and respecting them, even when we disagree. Taking account and repenting of historic injustices carried out by Christians also requires us to take a humble posture before people who reject the gospel. Entering into dialogue across religious boundaries is not an alternative to witness. It is, rather, an expression of witness, a sign that God listens, cares, and does not force, and an opportunity to articulate the meaning of the gospel for a particular audience. At its best, it complements but does not replace the invitation to faith.

Being the people of God in this world—that is the call of Jesus; that is the Jesus Way.

We are closer to the vision of Christ for the church when our common life as believers is focused on inviting others to know and follow the Savior. Evangelism is a corporate endeavor. Our life together is our gospel tract.[6]

Conclusion

The Jesus Way continues to be the same today as it has been for twenty centuries. We are invited to continue being a part of what God is doing in the world, as epitomized in the person of Jesus. The world has changed in many ways, but the basic issues persist. God is at work addressing the needs of the world. Humans are struggling and need God's grace to transform them. God works through Christians and churches, in the power of the Holy Spirit. We are invited to be active participants in that mission by living into God's future today.

Because we do mission in the way of Jesus, we will be concerned for the whole of human existence and for all of creation. We will invite others to follow Jesus and to enter into all that this implies. But we are also invited to be the salt of the earth. This means that we seek to be a blessing to all of humanity, including those who do not follow the Jesus Way.

Because of Jesus' invitation and call on our lives, we seek to live like Jesus in the power of the Holy Spirit. We take seriously the task of living into the mission of God as revealed in the way of Jesus.

The invitation for today continues to be the same: to join the Jesus Way of incarnational solidarity, to join the church in mission as it pursues shalom for all creation through the Spirit's loving power.

Glossary

atonement: The doctrine that focuses on how Jesus makes us "at one" with God. Some traditions focus their teaching on the atonement primarily on Jesus' death on the cross or on his incarnation. Anabaptists often teach that all of Jesus' story—his birth, life, death, and resurrection—unifies us to God.

contextualize, contextualization: The process by which the gospel is made at home in a given culture. Many missionaries are convinced that the gospel must undergo a process of contextualization to make sense in a new setting. Missionaries contribute to contextualization by learning about and from the cultures they are serving. Ultimately, it is the culture's own members, those who hear and respond to the gospel as good news, who will contextualize it.

gospel: The "good news" that God has acted decisively in Jesus Christ to redeem creation. God's action in Jesus makes available a new way of life, a new pattern of relationships, to humans now. We learn about this new way of life from Jesus' teachings and actions as we encounter them in the New Testament. When we receive the gospel, the Holy Spirit begins to transform our own speech and actions after Jesus' example, so that we ourselves might become witnesses to the gospel.

incarnation: The doctrine that God became human in and as Jesus of Nazareth, the first-century Palestinian Jew. Early Christian elaboration of this doctrine resulted in the doctrine of the Trinity: it is the Son, or Word, the second person of the Trinity, who is incarnate as Jesus. The doctrines of the incarnation and Trinity together teach that the God we meet in Jesus is the one God, the God of Israel.

mission: This term describes, in the first place, what God does to realize God's purposes for creation—the *missio Dei* (mission of God). In the second place, mission describes the church's efforts to join in what God is doing. The concept of mission (from Latin *missio*, "sending") is closely related to the concept of apostolicity—*apostolos* in Greek means "sent ones." The "apostolic" church is formed and guided by its sense of being sent, of having a divine mission. In recent decades the term *missional* has become popular to describe this orientation to mission, especially on a congregational level.

shalom: The word used in the Hebrew Scriptures to describe God's gift of peace, by which relations among humans, between humans and all of creation, and between creation and God are repaired and restored. Shalom was translated into Greek as *eirene*, and this term appears throughout the New Testament and is identified with Jesus. Jesus is the shalom of

God, so his followers can experience now the peace promised to all of creation.

sin: A theological term that describes how humans and other creatures miss the goals that God intends for us. Sin has social, ecological, and spiritual dimensions, so that any specific instance of sin can be assessed in terms of how it damages our communities, our bodies and the environment, and our relationship with God. Since Christians see Jesus as our best picture of healthy social, ecological, and spiritual relationships, sin can also be defined negatively in terms of falling short of Jesus' example of love and faithfulness.

Discussion and Reflection Questions

INTRODUCTION

1. What comes to mind when you hear the word *mission*? What kind of feelings does the word bring up for you? Excitement? Inspiration? Anger? Anxiety?

2. The authors say that the language of mission is "unavoidable" for describing what God is doing in the world and how the church is called to respond. Do you agree?

CHAPTER 1

1. The chapter begins with a story about John Perkins and Servant Partners. How did you feel about this story? Does it connect with your understanding of who Jesus was and what he did?

2. Think of some examples of the things that Jesus said and did. What can you learn from these examples about the mission of God and the mission of the church?

3. Read Luke 4:16-30. Who are the poor, the captives, the blind, the oppressed in your community? What might Jesus' ministry of liberation and healing look like in your community?

4. What is your view of the atonement? Do you agree with the authors' presentation of atonement and mission? How do you see the atonement relating to mission?

CHAPTER 2

1. Juan starts this chapter discussing how he learned about mission from an early age in his church. How did you learn about mission? Did you get a sense that it was something you were called to be involved in or not? Did you see mission modeled in healthy ways?

2. This chapter suggests that over the centuries, Christian mission has been implicated in imperialism, the Crusades, colonialism, and other injustices. Does this surprise you? Do you think churches can find ways to do mission that are less reliant on money and power? What might that look like?

3. Christian mission has often focused on converting people from other religions to Christianity. This chapter also discusses interreligious dialogue and learning from people of other religions as expressions of mission. How do you think Christians ought to relate to people from other religions?

4. Were you surprised to read about Christianity's demographic shift? How does this shift affect your

understanding of mission? Have you encountered missionaries from other parts of the world? What has that experience been like?

CHAPTER 3

1. This chapter begins with the story of Rosa del Carmen Ortez-Cruz requesting sanctuary from a Mennonite church in North Carolina. In what ways does Ortez-Cruz's request, and the church's response, resonate with your view of mission? Are there any ways that they challenge what you understand about mission?

2. Review the different images of the church in mission that are discussed in this chapter. Does one of these images best describe your own church and how it participates in God's mission? Do any of these images challenge your church to become more involved in mission?

3. The language of "sacraments" works differently in different Christian traditions. Does thinking of the gathered Christian community as itself a sacrament challenge your understanding of sacraments? Of mission?

CHAPTER 4

1. The stories of Matteo Ricci and Hudson Taylor show missionaries attempting to respect their host societies by adapting to their cultural norms. Are you aware of more recent examples of such adaptation? What are some of the benefits of this approach to mission? What are some of the dangers?

2. In what ways might the incarnation be a model for Christian intercultural mission? Can you think of an

example you've seen of intercultural mission done well? What made it successful?

3. How does the description of mission as service sound to you? What are some of the strengths and weaknesses of "service" language?

CHAPTER 5

1. Think about some of the major issues facing the church in the world. What do you see as the biggest challenges today? What gives you hope as the church and others seek to address those challenges?

2. How might acknowledgment of the history of Christian imperialism and violence shape your congregation's witness?

3. Read Jeremiah 29:4-9. Whom do you identify with most in the story? The exiles or the members of the dominant culture? How might your identity affect how you "seek the peace of the city"?

CONCLUSION

1. What do you think mission in the Jesus Way looks like? What is the Holy Spirit doing in your midst? How can you and your congregation join in?

Shared Convictions

Mennonite World Conference, a global community of Christian churches that facilitates community between Anabaptist-related churches, offers these shared convictions that characterize Anabaptist faith. For more on Anabaptism, go to ThirdWayCafe.com.

By the grace of God, we seek to live and proclaim the good news of reconciliation in Jesus Christ. As part of the one body of Christ at all times and places, we hold the following to be central to our belief and practice:

1. God is known to us as Father, Son and Holy Spirit, the Creator who seeks to restore fallen humanity by calling a people to be faithful in fellowship, worship, service and witness.

2. Jesus is the Son of God. Through his life and teachings, his cross and resurrection, he showed us how to be faithful disciples, redeemed the world, and offers eternal life.

3. As a church, we are a community of those whom God's Spirit calls to turn from sin, acknowledge Jesus Christ as Lord, receive baptism upon confession of faith, and follow Christ in life.

4. As a faith community, we accept the Bible as our authority for faith and life, interpreting it together under Holy Spirit guidance, in the light of Jesus Christ to discern God's will for our obedience.

5. The Spirit of Jesus empowers us to trust God in all areas of life so we become peacemakers who renounce violence, love our enemies, seek justice, and share our possessions with those in need.

6. We gather regularly to worship, to celebrate the Lord's Supper, and to hear the Word of God in a spirit of mutual accountability.

7. As a world-wide community of faith and life we transcend boundaries of nationality, race, class, gender and language. We seek to live in the world without conforming to the powers of evil, witnessing to God's grace by serving others, caring for creation, and inviting all people to know Jesus Christ as Saviour and Lord.

In these convictions we draw inspiration from Anabaptist forebears of the 16th century, who modelled radical discipleship to Jesus Christ. We seek to walk in his name by the power of the Holy Spirit, as we confidently await Christ's return and the final fulfillment of God's kingdom.

Adopted by Mennonite World Conference General Council, March 15, 2006

Notes

Introduction

1 Key terms appear in bold and are defined in the glossary.

Chapter 1

1 Donald B. Kraybill, *The Upside-Down Kingdom*, 25th anniv. ed. (Harrisonburg, VA: Herald Press, 2018).

2 John Driver, *Understanding the Atonement for the Mission of the Church* (Scottdale, PA: Herald Press, 1986).

Chapter 2

1 The book of Acts has twenty-eight chapters. In this understanding, what churches do in mission today is a clear continuation of Christ's command to his disciples and what the first generation of believers did after Christ's resurrection and return to glory.

2 Juan [John] Driver, *La fe a la periferia de la historia: Una historia del pueblo cristiano desde la perspectiva de los movimientos de Restauración y Reforma Radical* (Guatemala City: Ediciones SEMILLA, 1997), 55. Translation by Juan Martínez.

3 Nestorian Christians distinguished more sharply between Jesus' human and divine natures than did Nicene ("Catholic") Christians.

4 Lamin Sanneh, *Whose Religion Is Christianity? The Gospel beyond the West* (Grand Rapids, MI: Eerdmans, 2003).

5 In 2015, David Vine reported that "the United States . . . maintains
   nearly 800 military bases in more than 70 territories abroad—from
   giant 'Little Americas' to small radar facilities. Britain, France,
   and Russia, by contrast, have about 30 foreign bases combined."
   Vine, "Where in the World Is the US Military?" *Politico*, June
   2015, https://www.politico.com/magazine/story/2015/06/
   us-military-bases-around-the-world-119321.
6 Todd M. Johnson and Kenneth R. Ross, eds., *Atlas of Global
   Christianity* (Edinburgh: Edinburgh University Press, 2009).
7 Pew Research Center, "Global Christianity—A Report on the Size
   and Distribution of the World's Christian Population," December
   19, 2011, http://www.pewforum.org/files/2011/12/Christianity-
   fullreport-web.pdf.

Chapter 3

1 John Driver, *Images of the Church in Mission* (Scottdale, PA:
   Herald Press, 1997).
2 Walfred Fahrer, *Building on the Rock: A Biblical Vision of Being
   Church Together from an Anabaptist-Mennonite Perspective*
   (Scottdale, PA: Herald Press, 1995), 113.
3 Fahrer, 118–21.
4 David J. Bosch, *Transforming Mission: Paradigm Shifts in Theology
   of Mission* (Maryknoll, NY: Orbis, 1991).

Chapter 4

1 On the central role of women in the history of Christian mission,
   see Susan Smith, *Women in Mission: From the New Testament to
   Today* (Maryknoll, NY: Orbis, 2007).
2 Howard Taylor and Mary Taylor, *Hudson Taylor and the China
   Inland Mission: The Growth of a Work of God* (London: Morgan
   and Scott, 1920), 90–91.
3 See Wilbert R. Shenk, *Henry Venn: Missionary Statesman* (Eugene,
   OR: Wipf and Stock, 2006).
4 On the need for churches to be "self-theologizing," see David J.
   Bosch, *Transforming Mission: Paradigm Shifts in Theology of
   Mission* (Maryknoll, NY: Orbis, 1991).
5 In China, Venn's formula resulted in the establishment of the
   Three-Self Patriotic Movement, which is part of the official Protestant church recognized by the Chinese government.
6 See, for example, René Padilla, *Mission between the Times: Essays
   on the Kingdom* (Carlisle, UK: Langham, 2010).

Chapter 5

1 Jonathan J. Bonk, *Missions and Money: Affluence as a Missionary Problem . . . Revisited*, rev. ed. (Maryknoll, NY: Orbis, 2006).

2 Walter Wink, *Engaging the Powers: Discernment and Resistance in a World of Domination* (Minneapolis: Augsburg Fortress, 1992), 13–31.

3 Kim-Kwong Chan, "The Back to Jerusalem Movement: Mission Movement of the Christian Community in Mainland China," in *Mission Spirituality and Authentic Discipleship*, ed. Wonsuk Ma and Kenneth R. Ross (Oxford: Regnum, 2013), 172–92.

4 Samuel Escobar, *The New Global Mission: From Everywhere to Everyone* (Downers Grove, IL: InterVarsity, 2003).

5 Kimberlé Crenshaw developed the language of intersectionality to show how Black women's experience was ignored by both feminists—who focused on white women—and anti-racists—who focused on Black men. See her founding essay, "Demarginalizing the Intersection of Race and Sex: A Black Feminist Critique of Antidiscrimination Doctrine, Feminist Theory and Antiracist Politics," *University of Chicago Legal Forum* 1 (1989): 139–67.

6 Walfred Fahrer, *Building on the Rock: A Biblical Vision of Being Church Together from an Anabaptist-Mennonite Perspective* (Scottdale, PA: Herald Press, 1995), 106.

The Authors

Juan Francisco Martínez is president of Centro Hispano de Estudio Teológicos in Compton, California. Previously he was professor of Hispanic studies and pastoral leadership at Fuller Theological Seminary and rector of the Latin American Anabaptist Seminary (SEMILLA) in Guatemala

City. Martínez is an ordained Mennonite Brethren pastor and received his PhD in intercultural studies from Fuller. His academic work has focused on Latino Protestantism in the United States. Martínez is the author and editor of numerous books and articles.

Jamie Pitts is associate professor of Anabaptist theology at Anabaptist Mennonite Biblical Seminary, where he also serves as director of the Institute of Mennonite Studies and edits the journal *Anabaptist Witness*. His teaching focuses on theology and history, with an emphasis on global Anabaptist tra-

ditions past and present. His current research interests include pneumatology, baptism, and gender and sexuality. Pitts has degrees from New College at the University of Edinburgh and Fuller Theological Seminary.

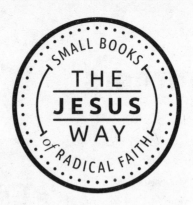

SMALL BOOKS
THE
JESUS
WAY
of RADICAL FAITH

HERALD
PRESS

www.HeraldPress.com. 1-800-245-7894